Working
HORSES

by Mary Packard

Consultant: Wayne Loch
University of Missouri

BEARPORT
PUBLISHING

New York, New York

Credits

Cover and Title Page, © Craig Aurness/Corbis; 4, © Private Collection, Peter Newark Western Americana/ The Bridgeman Art Library; 5, © Private Collection, Peter Newark Western Americana/The Bridgeman Art Library; 7, © Private Collection, Archives Charmet/The Bridgeman Art Library; 8, © Museum of the City of New York/Byron Collection/Getty Images/Newscom.com; 9, © North Wind/North Wind Picture Archives; 10, © Mary Evans Picture Library; 11, © Edwin Levick/Hulton Archive/Getty Images/Newscom. com; 12, © New York Public Library Picture Collection; 13, © Minnesota Historical Society/Corbis; 14, © The Bancroft Library. University of California, Berkeley; 15, Courtesy Library of Congress Prints and Photographs Division; 16, © W.A. Raymond/Corbis; 17, © Michael S. Lewis/Corbis; 18, © AP Images/Dean Musser Jr., Journal Gazette; 19, © Art Seitz/KPA/ZUMA Press/Newscom.com; 20, © Pixtal/SuperStock; 21, © Carson Ganci/Design Pics Inc./Alamy; 22, © AP Images/Uwe Lein; 23, © AP Images/Steve Parsons, PA; 24, © Joe Sohm/Visions of America, LLC/Alamy; 25, © Joe Sohm/Visions of America, LLC/Alamy; 26, © Hulton Archive/Getty Images/Newscom.com; 27, © Comstock Images/Alamy; 28, © Ian Dagnall/Alamy; 29TR, © Robert Maier/Animals Animals Earth Scenes; 29TL, © Bob Langrish; 29M, © Bob Langrish; 29BR, © Eunice Pearcy/Animals Animals Earth Scenes; 29BL, © Bob Langrish/DK Images.

Publisher: Kenn Goin
Project Editor: Lisa Wiseman
Creative Director: Spencer Brinker
Photo Researcher: Amy Dunleavy
Design: Stacey May

Library of Congress Cataloging-in-Publication Data

Packard, Mary.
 Working horses / by Mary Packard ; consultant, Wayne Loch.
     p. cm. — (Horse power)
 Includes bibliographical references and index.
 ISBN-13: 978-1-59716-403-0 (library binding)
 ISBN-10: 1-59716-403-8 (library binding)
 1. Horses—Juvenile literature. 2. Working animals—Juvenile literature. I. Title.
 II. Series: Horse power (Series)

SF302.P33 2007
636.1—dc22
                              2006031406

For more information, write to Bearport Publishing Company, Inc., 101 Fifth Avenue, Suite 6R, New York, New York 10003. Printed in the United States of America.

10 9 8 7 6 5 4 3 2 1

Contents

Special Delivery

On April 13, 1860, the people of Sacramento, California, gathered at the Pony Express station to wait for their mail. At the time, letters and newspapers traveled slowly across the country by **stagecoach**. The mail was the only way to find out news from family and friends who lived far away. However, by the time the mail arrived, the news was usually a month old.

Pony Express riders liked to ride a kind of horse called Mustangs because they were fast and did not get tired easily.

The youngest person to ride for the Pony Express was 11-year-old Charlie Miller. His horse was named Pole Star.

Could the Pony Express really deliver the mail faster? The people of Sacramento were about to find out. Soon everyone heard the sound of pounding **hooves**.

"Here they come!" someone shouted. "Hurray!" everyone cheered as a horse and rider sped into town. It was Billy Hamilton on a Mustang—the hardest-working **breed** of horse in the West.

A Pony Express rider arrives at a station.

A Celebration

The mail **route** stretched from Missouri to California. It was divided into stations where riders could stop to eat and get a new horse. New riders took over about every 75 to 100 miles (121 to 161 km). On April 13, 1860, Billy Hamilton had ridden all day in the rain.

The Pony Express ran between St. Joseph, Missouri, and Sacramento, California. There were about 150 to 190 stations in between the two cities.

Once in a while, a rider would fall asleep in the saddle! It's a good thing the Pony Express horses knew the route by heart.

When Billy arrived in Sacramento, he was greeted with a brass band and a big parade. It had taken more than 15 riders and 150 horses to carry the mail across the country by Pony Express. Horse by horse, rider by rider, the mail had traveled 1,966 miles (3,164 km). The trip had taken just ten days. Now that kind of speed was something to celebrate!

In Sacramento, Billy Hamilton was given a hero's welcome.

Draft Horses

For thousands of years, horses have been helping people. At first, working horses provided transportation for families and businesses. As the years passed, these animals also began to do work that humans or machines could not handle.

One kind of working horse is the **draft horse**. These animals are big and strong. They have wide chests and thick muscles. They can do heavy work such as pulling wagons and carriages.

Four horses pull a carriage full of people through the streets of New York in 1900.

A horse's height is measured in hands—from the ground to the top of its shoulder. Each hand equals four inches (10 cm).

Draft horses stand over 16 hands high and weigh between 1,400 and 2,000 pounds (635 and 907 kg). The largest breed of draft horse is the Shire. This horse was first **bred** by knights. Due to the heavy armor they wore during battles, knights needed extra-strong horses to carry them.

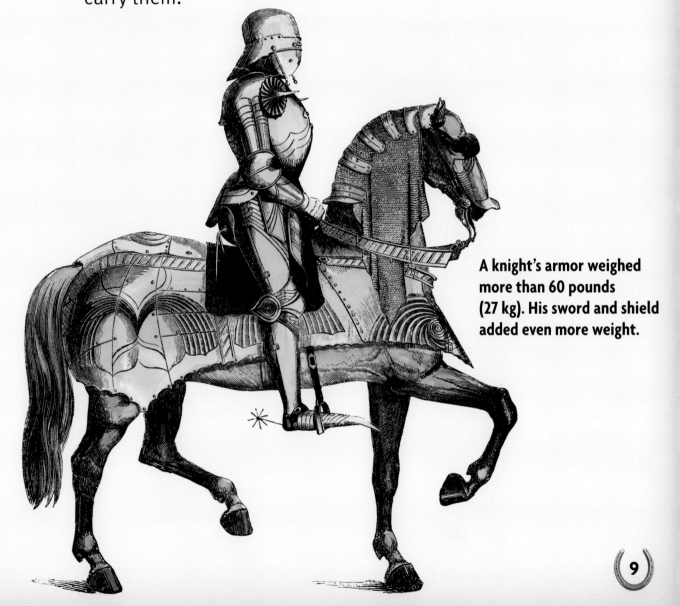

A knight's armor weighed more than 60 pounds (27 kg). His sword and shield added even more weight.

Pulling Their Weight

Shires have been working horses for hundreds of years. Before trucks were invented, people in cities depended on them for many jobs. These horses pulled wagonloads of wood and coal. They also pulled carts filled with milk and ice to people's homes.

These horses are pulling wagonloads full of goods.

Clydesdales are another popular type of draft horse. In the 1800s, before there were buses and taxis, these horses pulled carriages full of people to and from work. Their feet are as wide as dinner plates—just right for walking over slippery **cobblestones**.

Cars with motors were once called horseless carriages. When these machines were invented, people were not used to a **vehicle** moving without a horse pulling it.

A New York traffic jam about 100 years ago

Track Star

In the 1860s, the only way to get across the United States was by horse. If there was one thing the country needed, it was a railroad. In the early 1860s, workers finally started to build one. They were lucky to have a horse named Blind Tom to help them. He couldn't see, but in just a few years Blind Tom pulled 110,000 tons (99,790 metric tons) of **rails**.

Blind Tom (far left) hauls a boxcar full of rails.

For Native Americans, horses were the only means of transportation. When they first saw the train, they called it the Iron Horse.

The workers used the rails to build the train tracks. When the railroad was finished, in about 1869, the workers had a party to celebrate. Many important people came. However, just one horse was invited. After all, no one had done more to help build the railroad than Blind Tom.

These horses helped build a railroad in Minnesota in the 1800s.

To the Rescue!

Working horses are very brave animals. They have even been known to save lives. One day, in 1909, the fire bell sounded in the little town of New Bern, North Carolina. When Fred the fire horse heard the alarm, he left his **stall** and waited by the fire truck. Within seconds, an overhead **harness** dropped down on him.

Horses were once important members of fire departments.

Soon Fred was racing through the streets pulling the fire truck with its crew. Fred ran faster than he ever had before. When they got to the fire, Fred waited while the firefighters fought the blaze. He stood still as smoke and sparks swirled around his head. Everyone was saved that day because Fred got the truck to the fire in record time.

A horse-drawn fire truck races to a fire in 1912.

Fred was so beloved that when he died, the firefighters had him stuffed. He can still be seen at the Fireman's Museum in New Bern, North Carolina.

On the Farm

At one time, draft horses pulled all kinds of machines on farms. Fieldwork became easier after the **combine** was invented in the 1830s. Though the combine could do the work of many machines, it was very heavy. It took teams of super-strong draft horses called Percherons, to pull a huge combine through the fields.

A team of about 24 draft horses pulls a combine.

Today, combines run on gas. However, some farmers still keep a team of horses to do other work. There are times when only a horse can do a job. For example, in winter, it's hard to get machines or vehicles to start when it is 0°F (−17°C) outside. Even in the cold, horses can still pull a wagon full of grain to hungry cattle in the fields.

This rancher uses draft horses to help bring food to his cattle on a cold winter day.

Today the word "horsepower" is used to describe the amount of power a machine has.

Buggies

Today, draft horses are still used by the **Amish** to help with farming. The Amish don't use tractors or other **modern** machines. They rely on sturdy, strong, and gentle horses, such as Belgians, to help with fieldwork.

A team of horses helps an Amish farmer with his fieldwork.

The Amish don't own cars, trucks, or other vehicles. They travel in horse-drawn **buggies** to go to the store or visit friends. Horses called Standardbreds are most often used to pull the buggies around town.

To the Amish, horses are much-loved family members. When they become too old to work, these animals get to spend their **retirement** resting in grassy **pastures**.

Standardbred horses are used in **harness racing**. The Amish buy retired harness racers for their buggies.

A horse pulls an Amish buggy through snow in Ohio.

On the Ranch

Although they're called ponies, cow ponies are really full-sized Quarter Horses. Bred to run in short races, Quarter Horses are often found working on cattle ranches. In spring, they help round up newborn **calves** for branding. By fall, the calves have grown into cows and are ready to be sold. It takes a well-trained horse to **herd** the cattle to market.

A horse and cowboy work together to herd cattle in Wyoming.

Brands are marks that help a cowboy spot his own cow. The mark is burned into a cow's skin.

When a cow gets away from its herd, the cowboy steers his horse toward it. Then he sits back and lets the horse take over. The animal follows the cow's every move. He shadows it with quick twists and turns. The horse seems to know what the cow will do before he makes his move! Before long, the cow is back with the herd.

These horses carefully watch over the cattle during a cattle drive.

Horse Play

Many working horses have jobs entertaining people. These animals are often the highlight of a circus. During daring performances, draft horses are used to pull colorful floats around the ring. Riders do tricks on the bare backs of other horses. Some horses show off fancy moves.

A circus horse has to be strong to hold two performers on his back.

The most famous performing horses of all are called Lipizzaners. These animals were first bred in Spain. They gracefully march with their feet lifted high to the sound of music. They sway from side to side. They rise up on their **hind** legs and leap through the air. The horses make the moves look easy. However, each step takes great strength and years of practice.

A Lipizzaner practicing a jump

Newborn Lipizzaners can be brown or black. Almost all turn white when they are adults.

Horses on Parade

Though horses are very brave animals, they can be easily **startled**. Their **instinct** is to run from danger. For this reason it can take months to get a horse ready to work in a parade.

These horses were trained to stay calm around crowds.

Sudden movements, such as waving flags, can frighten a horse. These animals are also scared by loud horns, popping balloons, and cheering crowds. Their trainers get them used to these situations one at a time. When a horse is no longer frightened of a waving flag, the trainer then teaches her to be calm around large groups of people. Little by little the horse becomes used to new sights and sounds.

A horse's hooves are like human fingernails. They are growing all the time.

These horses pull an old-fashioned fire engine during a parade in California.

Gentle Giants

For 6,000 years, horses have worked with humans. These animals have spent endless hours working in fields. They also helped people travel farther and faster than they ever could on their own.

Teams of horse-drawn wagons traveling through Boise, Idaho, in 1885.

Horses usually live for about 20 to 25 years. There are some horses that can live to age 30.

Working horses have not only assisted with everyday chores. They have also provided endless hours of entertainment for people by performing in parades and circuses.

Horses are among our most helpful and loyal friends. It can even be said that horses have changed history—for the better!

Just the Facts

- The fastest Pony Express ride took 7 days and 17 hours. It began in St. Joseph, Missouri, and ended in Sacramento, California. The rider was carrying the speech made by Abraham Lincoln on the day he became president in 1861.

- Horses do not run as fast when they carry heavy loads. For this reason, Pony Express riders could not weigh more than 125 pounds (57 kg).

- A Shire named Samson, born in 1846, grew to be 21.25 hands tall. He weighed 3,360 pounds (1,524 kg).

- In 1872, a fire broke out in Boston. Why did it get out of control? A flu struck all of the city's horses. Very few of them were healthy enough to pull fire engines to the blaze.

- Most **loggers** use trucks to carry trees, that have been cut down, out of the woods. However, some loggers prefer to use horses for the job. Horses can fit in spaces too small for big trucks. They also do not pollute the air.

A street sign found in an Amish community

Common Breeds

Working Horses

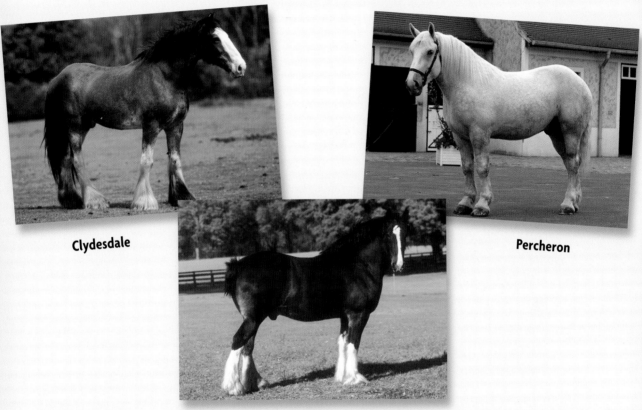

Clydesdale

Percheron

Shire

Standardbred

Mustang

Glossary

Amish (AH-mish) a religious group of people who live very simply without the use of modern technology, such as cars

bred (BRED) raised

breed (BREED) a type of horse

buggies (BUHG-eez) light carriages with four wheels pulled by horses

calves (KAVZ) very young cattle

cobblestones (KOB-uhl-stohnz) round rocks that were once used to build streets and roads

combine (KAHM-bine) a farm machine that cuts and separates grain and other crops

draft horse (DRAFT HORSS) a large horse that is bred to do hard and heavy work

harness (HAR-niss) straps that connect horses to the things they pull, such as wagons

harness racing (HAR-niss RAYSS-ing) a type of race where the jockey sits in a light two-wheeled cart

herd (HURD) to make people or animals move together

hind (HINDE) the back

hooves (HOOVZ) a horse's feet

instinct (IN-stingkt) a natural way of acting that an animal does not have to learn

loggers (LOG-urz) people who cut down trees to clear land

modern (MOD-urn) having to do with the present; up-to-date

pastures (PASS-churz) grass-covered fields where animals can graze

rails (RAYLZ) steel bars used to form a train track

retirement (re-TIRE-ment) the period in one's life when one stops working, usually because of age

route (ROOT) the road a person follows to get from one place to another

stagecoach (STAYJ-*kohch*) a large carriage pulled by horses that travels long distances

stall (STAWL) a small indoor place, usually in a stable or a barn, where a horse is kept

startled (STAR-tuhld) frightened or surprised

vehicles (VEE-uh-kuhlz) something that carries goods or people from place to place

Bibliography

Bowers, Steve, and Marlen Steward. *Farming with Horses.* St. Paul, MN: MBI Publishing Company (2006).

Moody, Ralph. *Riders of the Pony Express.* Lincoln, NE: University of Nebraska Press (2004).

Patent, Dorothy Hinshaw. *Draft Horses.* New York: Holiday House (1986).

Read More

Coerr, Eleanor. *Buffalo Bill and the Pony Express.* New York: HarperCollins (1995).

Lundell, Margo. *Harold Roth's Big Book of Horses.* New York: Grosset & Dunlop (1987).

Peterson, Cris. *Horsepower: The Wonder of Draft Horses.* Honesdale, PA: Boyds Mills (2001).

Learn More Online

To learn more about working horses, visit
www.bearportpublishing.com/HorsePower

Index

About the Author

Mary Packard lives in Northport, New York. She has written more than 200 children's books. Her favorites are the ones about animals.

5/07